Customer Service
Excellence

Customer Service Excellence

DEBRA J. MacNEILL

The Business Skills Express Series

McGraw-Hill

New York   San Francisco   Washington, D.C.   Auckland   Bogotá   Caracas
Lisbon   London   Madrid   Mexico City   Milan   Montreal   New Delhi
San Juan   Singapore   Sydney   Tokyo   Toronto

McGraw-Hill

A Division of The McGraw·Hill Companies

© 1994 by the McGraw-Hill Companies, Inc.

This publication is designed to provide accurate and authoritative information in regard to the subject matter covered. It is sold with the understanding that neither the author nor the publisher is engaged in rendering legal, accounting, or other professional service. If legal advice or other expert assistance is required, the services of a competent professional person should be sought.

From a Declaration of Principles jointly adopted by a Committee of the American Bar Association and a Committee of Publishers.

Library of Congress Cataloging-in-Publication Data

MacNeill, Debra J.
   Customer service excellence / Debra J. MacNeill.
     p.   cm.—(Business skills express)
   ISBN 1-55623-969-6
   1. Customer service. I. Title.
  HF5415.5.M13 1994
  658.8'12—dc20
                        93–6

Printed in the United States of America
  12 13 14 15 MAL/MAL 0 9 8 7

PREFACE

Customer service is a pressing issue in this decade. In the ever-expanding market of today's competitive industries, few topics have received as much attention, both in time and money, as the need to have excellent service personnel. Providing quality service is a skill that will set you and your company apart from your competitors.

Customer Service Excellence is designed to build and maintain the critical skills necessary to be a dynamic and successful service professional. The front line individuals who work with customers every day will gain insight on customer behavior and attitudes and will develop strategies to create positive customer relationships in every encounter. Whether you are newly employed or a veteran with years of customer interactions, you will learn a practical approach to the thorny issue of customer dissatisfaction that will save you time and energy. Managers can use this guide as a part of their new-employee orientation and training programs or as a refresher course to keep service personnel focused on the company's goals and objectives.

Start by taking the Self-Assessment. This will quickly assess your customer service skills and knowledge and serve as a platform for your training. Work through the seven chapters at your own pace. The book presents opportunities for you to examine your own behavior, the key issues of your business, and to profile the customer interactions you encounter on a daily basis. Chapter 7 will help you to rate your own customer service skills. Prepare the action plan and you will be on your way to becoming a real service professional. Take the Post-Test when you have completed all the activities; it will reaffirm your mastery of the material.

Use the Skill Maintenance checklist to maintain your momentum after completing your training. Make a commitment to measure your success on an ongoing basis by completing the checklist at regular intervals. You and your customers will reap the rewards.

Debra J. MacNeill

ABOUT THE AUTHOR

Debra J. MacNeill is principal and founder of DJM Consulting in Boston, Massachusetts. Her training specialties include designing and implementing customer service programs for banking, travel, and other industries. As a training manager for the Bank of Boston, Ms. MacNeill designed retail training programs with a focus on customer service. In addition, she has conducted numerous workshops on product knowledge and sales throughout the country.

About the Business Skills Express Series

This expanding series of authoritative, concise, and fast-paced books delivers high quality training on key business topics at a remarkably affordable cost. The series will help managers, supervisors, and front line personnel in organizations of all sizes and types hone their business skills while enhancing job performance and career satisfaction.

Business Skills Express books are ideal for employee seminars, independent self-study, on-the-job training, and classroom-based instruction. Express books are also convenient-to-use references at work.

CONTENTS

Self-Assessment

Providing excellent customer service is both challenging and rewarding. Use this self-assessment to assess the way you presently handle your customers. The chapters that follow will confirm your service expertise or shed light on some new ways of effectively working with people.

	Almost Always	Sometimes	Almost Never
1. I don't let my personal feelings get in the way of serving my customers.	_____	_____	_____
2. I follow up with customers who have encountered problems with products or services.	_____	_____	_____
3. I thank my customers for their business.	_____	_____	_____
4. I make an effort to build partnerships with the people who work with me.	_____	_____	_____
5. I listen when customers complain.	_____	_____	_____
6. I explain product and service features using words that my customers understand.	_____	_____	_____
7. I am firm, but gentle, when saying no to a customer.	_____	_____	_____
8. I take the time to review my interactions with customers and learn from my mistakes.	_____	_____	_____
9. I look for solutions to problems with my customers.	_____	_____	_____
10. I communicate effectively over the telephone.	_____	_____	_____

1

Building a Foundation

This chapter will help you to:

- Explain your responsibility to your customers.
- Define what customers expect from you.
- Examine the factors that lead to customer dissatisfaction.
- Explore the positive consequences of handling challenging customers.

"This is going to take forever," thinks Charles Greenfield. "Why aren't the other cash registers open?" He glances over to the other lanes where two salespeople, engaging in conversation, seem unconcerned with the lengthening lines.

José Santiago, the store manager, trapped by Sonia Washington, a customer with a product complaint, looks helplessly toward the other customers. Sonia continues, "I turned it on and the handle broke off. I only used it twice. Don't you think I deserve a refund?"

"Ma'am, I'm sorry, but I have to get the other lanes open," José pleads. "Why don't you take this up with customer service?" He points in the direction of the rear of the store as he speeds off toward the checkout counters. Sonia looks down at the box in her hands, shakes her head, and leaves the store. When she gets back on the Senior Shuttle she recounts the whole story to her friends. "I won't be shopping there again," she announces. "Their prices might be right, but the employees are just plain rude." All 10 heads on the shuttle nod in agreement.

Meanwhile, Charles, still in line, heaves a sigh. "I don't have time for this, Marge and the boys are waiting for me to take them to the beach. I'll just stop at the convenience mart on the way." ■

WHAT IS YOUR RESPONSIBILITY?

The first step toward working with a challenging customer is to understand your responsibility to that customer. Every interaction between you and a customer involves an internal contract.

When you accepted your position, you agreed to provide a product or service that the public needs or wants in return for some monetary compensation from your employer. Perhaps you went through an internal training program that identified the features and benefits of the product your company provides, or perhaps you were coached on the job about how to provide service to your customer. Regardless, every time you approach a customer, in person or over the telephone, your interaction will be affected by personal guidelines that you have established over time through working with people.

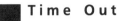 ## Time Out

Take a few minutes to reflect on past and present customer interactions. How do you define your responsibility to your customers? What will you do for them as you go through a typical interaction? Where does your responsibility end and the customer's begin?

I am responsible for providing my customers with . . .

_____

_____

_____

_____

In doing so, I will . . .

_____

_____

_____

_____

It's up to the customer to . . .

_____

_____

_____

_____

You have just outlined your internal contract with your customers. This contract creates the foundation on which you will build a relationship with everyone who enters your place of business. It may include time frames, such as "I will answer the telephone within three rings" or "I will apologize to any customer that has to wait in line longer than five minutes." Keep in mind that your internal contracts need to be flexible. Sometimes it doesn't make sense to create a rigid contract at the expense of good service. You may find that a personal greeting has become standard, such as "Welcome to Marty's. I hope you enjoy the food." Undoubtedly, these habits have evolved over time through trial and error.

The Basics

How you define excellent customer service depends on what product or service you offer the public and on what type of customer services you have to offer. However, some practices are a function of common sense and courtesy. Basically, you are responsible for providing your customers with:

- A pleasant, friendly greeting.
- A positive and helpful attitude.
- A professional and accurate business transaction.
- An apology for any delay.
- A quick resolution to problems.
- A sincere thank-you for their business.

It sounds simple? Well, it truly is simple. As a provider of goods or services—whether you work in a grocery store, a local bank, a lawyer's office, or a computer store—you are responsible for treating your customers with service that reflects a basic respect for their patronage. As you will discover, customers ultimately determine the success or failure of any business enterprise. If you don't give customers what they want, when they want it, in a positive and helpful manner, they will take their business elsewhere. Some astonishing statistics reveal just how important your role is in customer service. Customers surveyed as to why they took their business elsewhere revealed the following:

3 percent moved.

5 percent developed other relationships.

9 percent left for competitive reasons.

14 percent were dissatisfied with the product.

68 percent left because of an attitude of indifference toward the customer by the owner, manager, or some other employee.

To avoid projecting an indifferent attitude to your customers, you need to examine who your customers are, what they want, and how you can provide them with what they need.

WHAT DO YOUR CUSTOMERS EXPECT?

Customers come in a variety of shapes and sizes. Naturally people walk through your door for a purpose. The sign outside your establishment is the first clue to what's inside—maybe the windows display some of your goods or the advertisement in last night's

newspaper caught their eye. No matter what caused them to enter or call your place of business, while they are within your boundaries, they are affected not only by your courtesy but by intangible qualities that will shape their perceptions of you and the business or service you offer.

Meeting Expectations

Whether your business is widgets, wedding invitations, or weight control, your customers want to be listened to, understood, cared for, and treated fairly, intelligently, and individually. They expect that you and your business satisfy certain requirements.

Quality	Expectation
Reliability	Performance is consistent; customers can depend on having access to the business or service when they need it, not when it's convenient; promises are kept; things are done right the first time; things are done on time.
Credibility	Materials are genuine; claims are honest; reputation is based on fact, not fiction; products are safe; salespeople are trustworthy; problems will be handled directly.
Appeal	Prices are fair; premises are clean, bright, and free of clutter; salespeople are dressed appropriately and conduct business professionally; products are displayed attractively; printed materials are neat and easy to read; telephone conversations are pleasant and convey accurate information.
Responsiveness	Business is easily accessible; salespeople are helpful and readily available; service is quick; communication is prompt; problems are solved in a reasonable time frame; customers are kept informed of the process.
Concern	Customers are treated as individuals; salespeople are empathetic; problems are viewed as opportunities to demonstrate reliability and credibility.

Perception Is Everything

A customer's perception is the key to service quality. A philosopher once said, "What concerns me is not the way things are, but the way people think things are." The same is true today. If what you do is not perceived as valuable by the customer, then it is not valuable. Managing customer expectations will lead you down the path to service excellence.

Who Are Your Customers?

Before you can tackle the issue of how to handle challenging customers, you need to know who your customers are and specifically what they want from your business or service. You may have received a package from your marketing department that gives the demographics of people who buy your goods and services. That will give you information about your typical customer's age, sex, income, education, and so forth. But you need to look beyond the statistics and ask yourself, "Who are my customers?" With this question in mind, complete the following survey.

YOU AND YOUR CUSTOMER SURVEY

1. Describe the customers you see or hear from most often.

_____

_____

_____

2. What do they want from you or your business?

_____

_____

_____

3. What can you offer them?

_____

_____

_____

4. How can you add value to your customers' experience?

_____

_____

_____

The Inside Story.   As you think about your customers, consider this. You work with people inside your organization every day—the receptionist, the floor manager, your boss. You interact with other departments regularly—human resources, payroll, and shipping. At times you depend on them to provide you with a service or product that you need in order to provide your customers with what they expect. At other times, they need you to supply them with information or goods that will enable them to perform their functions. You are both the giver and receiver of internal services. The people and departments you work with are as much your customers as the ones outside your organization who pay for your service or product. Service standards apply to all your customers, inside and out. Remember, the one you serve may be serving you someday.

Focus on the Positive.   Creating positive experiences for your inside business associates contributes to your ability to meet the expectations of your outside customers. Try the You and Your Customer survey again, this time with an eye toward those you serve inside your organization.

YOU AND YOUR INSIDE CUSTOMER SURVEY

1. On what departments and/or people do you depend to provide you with the services or products you need to satisfy your outside customers?

_____

_____

_____

2. What do you need from them?

_____

_____

_____

3. What departments and/or people depend on you to provide goods or services that enable them to do their job?

_____

_____

_____

4. What do they need from you?

_____

_____

_____

Review your answers to the two customer surveys periodically as you go through the rest of this book to be sure you are aware what your customers expect from you.

WHAT CREATES DISSATISFACTION?

In Chapters 3 and 4, we'll probe deeper into how to discover what your customers want. Now, let's examine what our customers don't want, what makes them unhappy, and what we can learn from listening to customer complaints.

Focus on your most recent experience as a customer that left you with a feeling of great satisfaction. It might have involved a purchase you made or an encounter you had. Whatever you choose, it should be an experience that you could describe as outstanding. Without detail, list the characteristics of the encounter that describe the service. What made the experience memorable?

_____

_____

_____

_____

Now recall the most recent encounter you had as a customer that left you with a feeling of great dissatisfaction. What was the cause of that dissatisfaction?

_____

_____

_____

_____

The Dissatisfaction Equation

Was the satisfactory experience or the unsatisfactory experience easier to remember, describe, and record? Chances are you clearly remember the details of the bad experience. Perhaps you immediately told your family and friends the story of how you were mistreated, made to wait, or totally ignored. You were angry because your expectations were not met, and you needed to vent your frustrations. It's not hard to see why customers whose expectations are not met tell their tale of woe to at least 8 other people; 20 percent will tell as many as 20 others.

Common Customer Complaints. Take a moment to think about what causes your customers to be unhappy, disappointed, or dissatisfied. List the 10 complaints you hear most often.

Top 10 Customer Complaints

1. _____

2. _____

3. _____

4. _____

5. _____

1

6. _____

7. _____

8. _____

9. _____

10. _____

In general, customer dissatisfaction stems from:

- Promises not delivered.
- Service that was rude and inefficient.
- Conflicting messages from employees.
- Feelings of being victimized by the business or operation.
- Misinformation from an employee.
- Delays and long waits.
- Lack of communication between parties in dispute.
- Treatment as being uninformed, wrong, or unimportant.
- Defective or inferior products.
- Feelings of being dismissed or discounted by the personnel.
- Business integrity or honesty that was questionable.

Who Profits?   You may not have any control over how your customers react to dissatisfaction. Later in this book, you will learn how to diffuse potentially explosive situations with dissatisfied customers. Now begin thinking about how providing excellent customer service can profit you and your organization. Look again at your list of top 10 customer complaints. Which items can you control? Probably all of them, to one extent or another. Understanding what the customer wants and doesn't want, and satisfying those needs with quality products and excellent services, will give you and your organization a competitive edge in the marketplace of the 1990s.

WHAT CAN YOU LEARN FROM CUSTOMER COMPLAINTS?

You may be surprised to know that you can learn something from listening to customer complaints and that savvy and successful businesses actually invite customers to find their faults. Consider this: 96 percent of customers with complaints never make those complaints known to the business.

Why do you think it is dangerous to have all those silent, dissatisfied customers? Write down your responses.

_____

_____

_____

_____

Some of your answers probably focus on the possibility that customers will take their business elsewhere, quietly, and quite likely, permanently. *Statistics indicate that 91 percent of dissatisfied customers slip quietly away, never to return.*

In dollars and cents alone, this is a startling percentage. Figure the lifetime value of just one of your customers using the following formula.

Individual Customer Value

Amount of money spent annually $_____ × _____ length (in years) of relationship = $_____ lifetime value of the customer.

Also, consider the fact that it costs six times more to acquire a new customer than it does to keep an existing one. The value of keeping customers happy goes up exponentially. Just one negative customer experience can eliminate a customer for life. In fact, companies that score high on customer satisfaction and quality of service also show a better return on sales and gain market share.

Opportunity Knocks

The value of listening to customer complaints lies in discovering why the customer is dissatisfied and in understanding what would make the situation better from the customer's perspective. This gives you an all-important opportunity to focus quality improvement efforts where they will count the most. Reflect for a moment on the encounter, related earlier, that left you dissatisfied.

Did you complain?

If you did, was the situation resolved to your satisfaction?

1

Was the problem resolved quickly?

Are you still a customer of that company?

If you answered yes to all these questions, you are among the majority. In truth, among customers whose complaints are resolved quickly to their satisfaction, 95 percent continue to do business with the company. However, it may take a dozen positive customer service encounters to overcome one negative experience.

Fear Not

Do not be afraid of complainers. If handled properly, they may become your most loyal customers. An open and honest dialogue with a customer who has legitimate concerns about the quality of your product or service can open your eyes to their unmet expectations. What you should fear are the silent masses who never tell you what went wrong and simply take their business around the corner.

That's why the most successful businesses actually invite customer comments. Comment cards tucked in with bills, in hotel rooms, and on restaurant tables are one way to check how well you are doing in the area of service. A simple, "how was everything?" may open the door to a conversation of value.

Remember, listening to customer complaints can:

- Build better customer relations.
- Maintain an existing customer base.
- Reduce the cost of earning market share.
- Improve the quality of your product or service.
- Increase your market share and profitability.

Now it's time to put what you have learned in this chapter into practice.

Joan Shapiro walks into the local video store to rent a movie for her date tonight. The store is quiet and the salesperson is stocking the shelves. Joan approaches the computerized information counter to check whether the title she is looking for is in the store. She types T-E-R-M-I-N-A-T-O-R into the machine. The computer lists several copies as IN under "Action/Adventure" in aisle nine. Joan walks down aisle nine scanning the shelves for the movie she knows her boyfriend, Steven Mellon, wants to see. "He'll be so pleased when I tell him!" she thinks to herself. She grabs a copy and brings it to the counter to pay.

Later that night with Steven at her side, Joan puts the video in the VCR and pushes PLAY. Nothing happens. She pushes it harder this time. Still nothing. Steven heaves a sigh and asks, "What's wrong?" "I don't know," Joan says impatiently. Then she ejects the video only to find that the tape is broken. "I can't believe it," she cries in exasperation, "I'm going to call the video store right now!"

The clerk answers the phone after several rings. Joan explains the situation carefully and asks if there is another copy of *Terminator* in the store. "Look, lady," says the clerk, "it's Friday night. Do you really expect that a film as popular as *Terminator* is still going to be here? Bring it back and pick out something else." ■

Review & Practice

Answer the following questions.

1. What did Joan want, need, or expect?

_____

_____

_____

2. How is Joan feeling after her phone conversation with the salesperson at the video store?

_____

_____

_____

3. If Joan were to bring this matter to the attention of the store manager, what might she complain about?

_____

_____

_____

4. What are the video store's responsibilities to Joan?

_____

_____

_____

5. What could the video store's staff have done to avoid leaving Joan dissatisfied?

_____

_____

_____

Chapter Checkpoints

✓ Understand your responsibilities to your customers.

✓ Build partnerships with associates inside the company.

✓ Strive to meet customer expectations.

✓ Understand your customers—who they are and what they need.

✓ Identify customer complaints and listen to the valuable information they offer.

2 | Understanding Your Customers

This chapter will help you to:

- Identify what motivates customer behavior.
- Respond positively to customer needs.
- Identify the role emotions play in customer behavior.

Captain Elizabeth Breslin eased the plane onto the runway smoothly and efficiently. "Ahhh," she thought to herself, "another successful flight—and a half-hour before our estimated time of arrival. We're better than the on-time airline. We're the ahead-of-time airline!"

The passengers collected their gear from the overhead compartments as the flight attendants secured the doorways and made the cabin ready for exit. Tired from the long flight, but still smiling, flight attendant Tony Coles readied himself to bid the passengers farewell.

Mina Katz, in 4C, looked out the window and groaned. She was on her way to her first important board meeting in Chicago, and her nerves were shot. "Oh, great," she moaned, "now I get to spend an extra 30 minutes in this little airport before my connecting flight." She collected her briefcase and purse and started for the door.

Tony beamed at Mina as he neared the door and picked up the microphone for his final announcement on the public address system. "Thank you for flying Nuflight! We are pleased to provide you with excellent service. Enjoy your stay in Amity or have a safe and pleasant journey to your final destination. We look forward to flying with you in the near future."

2

Mina dropped her briefcase at Tony's feet and loudly proclaimed, "This is an abomination! Why can't you people ever get it right? Do you really think it's excellent service to strand us here in Amity for longer than we have to be? Next time, I'll fly the on-time airline." ■

WHAT MOTIVATES CUSTOMER BEHAVIOR?

In Chapter 1, you took a look at what causes your customers to be dissatisfied with your product or service. You learned what customers expect from your business and what can happen if their wants and needs are not met. To prevent dissatisfied customers from taking their business elsewhere, you need to dig a little deeper into what motivates customer behavior.

Five Basic Needs

The best place to begin to understand how customer needs affect behavior is with Abraham Maslow's hierarchy of needs theory. Maslow identified five levels of human needs: physiological, safety/security, social, esteem, and self-actualization (see figure and table).

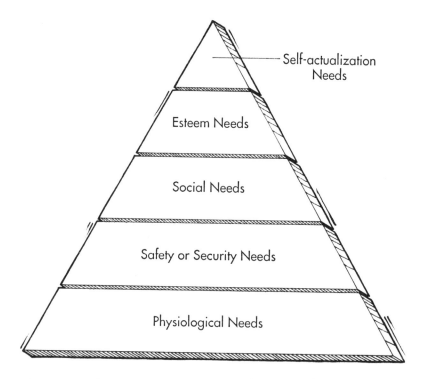

Level	Needs
Physiological	The basic human elements of survival—food, shelter, air, and water.
Safety/security	Protection from physical danger or threat; psychological safety.
Social	Friendship; a feeling of belonging; acceptance by the group.
Esteem	Self-respect; self-confidence; competence; recognition; appreciation; status.
Self-actualization	Making a lasting and significant contribution; maximizing personal growth and potential.

According to Maslow, human behavior is influenced by the strongest or most immediate need. Maslow's theory suggests that when an individual's needs at any one level are satisfied, he or she is free to move to the next level and begin seeking ways to meet the needs of that level, and so on. A number of factors can contribute to where an individual is on the hierarchy of needs at any point in time—work, family, friends, economics, or education. When conditions change, needs probably change. A student's needs may change after graduation from school; a husband's and wife's needs may change after the birth of a baby; a senior citizen's needs may change after the death of a spouse. A person's position on the hierarchy of needs is fluid and can move up or down depending on a variety of factors.

The Customer's Perspective

Although Maslow's theory was not designed to explain consumer behavior in a business context, it is nonetheless useful to adapt the theory to such a purpose.

Let's put the theory into practice from the customer's perspective. Think about all the customers you see or hear from on a regular basis, and look at the following chart. When a customer walks into or calls your place of business, he or she will be concerned with different aspects of your product or service depending on his or her level of need. In the following table a few possible concerns are outlined for each need level.

Level	Concerns
Physiological needs	Are the prices fair and reasonable? Are the goods durable? Does the company offer warranties or guarantees on products and services? Will the product or service be harmful or damaging to me or my family?
Safety/security needs	Is the business in a safe location? Is parking available? Is the business open during hours convenient for me? What happens if I need to speak to someone after hours?

Level	Concerns
Social needs	Are the employees friendly? Do they make customers feel comfortable? Will the product affect my ability to make or keep friends? How many other people that I know use the product or service?
Esteem needs	Do the employees treat customers as individuals? Will others recognize this as an intelligent purchase? Do the employees demonstrate appreciation for my patronage? Will I gain status by using the product or service?
Self-actualization needs	How will this product add value to my experience or improve my understanding of the world? Is the company willing to customize the product or service to suit my particular situation?

One Step Beyond

Let's take this one step further. Imagine for a moment that you are a customer. You walk into a local laundromat with items to be laundered. What is your need level and what are your concerns if:

1. You are a young, single mother with two toddlers in tow and lunch to prepare?

_____

_____

2. You are a widow and live alone?

_____

_____

3. You are a working professional with several very expensive designer outfits to be cleaned?

_____

_____

4. You are a graduate student writing your final thesis?

_____

_____

5. You are new to the area and unsure about the neighborhood?

_____

_____

Given such little information, it is possible your answers may vary, but as a jumping-off point, consider the following possibilities.

2

1. Young, single mother—possibly at the level of physiological needs, concerned with feeding her two children and spending as little time and money as possible at the laundromat.

2. Widow—possibly at the level of social needs, concerned with opportunities to interact with others and to spend time outside the home.

3. Working professional—possibly at the esteem level, concerned with getting the best care for her expensive clothes.

4. Graduate student—possibly at the self-actualization level, concerned with getting the laundry done quickly so he can return to his work.

5. New to the area—possibly at the safety level, concerned with finding a laundromat in a safe and convenient area.

You may be able to recognize many other need levels and concerns for the characters above. The purpose of the exercise is to think about the customers you see every day as individuals—what may they need from you and your business and how do their needs motivate their interactions with you?

HOW DO YOU RESPOND POSITIVELY

Understanding what motivates your customers is the first step in planning a strategy to respond positively to each customer during every encounter. At several points during an interaction with a customer, you will have an opportunity to shape a positive experience for that customer and to earn that customer's loyalty. Navigating through these points of encounter can be tricky, especially if you lose sight of what the customer needs, but if you keep focused and view the situation through the customer's eyes, you can steer a steady course.

Instances of Impact

In measuring the success of a customer encounter, you must consider moments during the encounter that provide you with an opportunity to add value to the customer's experience. Instances of impact often occur from the moment customers walk through the door until the door closes behind them or from the moment the telephone rings in your office until you replace the receiver in its cradle.

What do your customers see when they enter your place of business?

Are the shelves fully stocked with merchandise?

Are the aisles clearly marked and kept free of clutter?

Is there enough service staff to handle customer questions and to process purchases through the checkout counters?

What is the general atmosphere in your office or outlet?

Is it quiet and dignified?

Does it impart an aura of confidence and professionalism?

Is it casual and friendly?

What about telephone interactions?

Are customers greeted pleasantly?

If they are placed on hold, how long do they wait?

Is there background music or empty air on the line?

Pay Attention to the Big Four

To create positive customer encounters, you need to focus on the instances of impact that occur every time a customer does business with you. In general, customers are affected by a mix of four factors:

1. Physical plant.
2. Employees.
3. Product or service.
4. Atmosphere.

Your customer experiences your business through all four factors. Remember what you learned in the previous chapter about customer expectations? Customer expectations contribute to the customer's perception of the quality of your product or service. Put expectations together with reality so you can appreciate the customer's viewpoint. Complete the following chart as a tool to help you reflect on the four factors of impact. Identify specific aspects of your business that enhance the impact and those that may detract from it. Consider the following questions as you complete the chart:

Physical plant: Is it clean, bright, well-organized, and in a convenient and safe location?

Employees: Are they neatly and professionally dressed, well-groomed, and helpful?

Product or service: Is it reliable, priced fairly, and well-stocked?

Atmosphere: Are customers treated with respect? Is service friendly and efficient? Is the company's reputation favorable?

Impact Factor	Customer Expectations	Specific Enhancers	Specific Detractors
Physical plant			
Employees			
Product or service			
Atmosphere			

Focus on the Positive.   Use the information from your completed chart to plan ways to positively affect every customer interaction. Remember to focus on those areas you consider enhancers and work to reduce the detractors. For example, if a warm greeting enhances the encounter between employees and customers in your estimation, be sure to continue to greet your customers warmly. If a messy desk seems to have a negative impact on customer encounters, take time to straighten your work area and strive to keep it that way.

WHAT ROLE DO EMOTIONS PLAY?

Many psychologists believe human emotions fall into one of four categories—happy, sad, angry, and scared. Each emotion has degrees of intensity. However, when boiled down to the lowest common denominator, all human emotions can be categorized into one of the basic four. Look at the following chart for examples of the range for each emotional state.

Emotional State	Range of Intensity
Happy	Satisfied, ecstatic, joyous, pleased, radiant, ebullient, excited, elated, euphoric, or enthusiastic.
Sad	Depressed, despondent, gloomy, dejected, discouraged, miserable, hopeless, or distressed.
Angry	Irate, incensed, hostile, belligerent, cranky, grouchy, annoyed, furious, upset, or provoked.
Scared	Nervous, anxious, concerned, worried, aghast, petrified, paranoid, terrified, or threatened.

Your Role

Your role as a customer service provider is to ensure that your customers are happy with your product or service. Customers want to be pleased with their purchases, they want to enjoy their encounter with you and your business, and they want to feel good about themselves when the interaction is over. Anything that causes the customer to be sad, angry, or scared as a result of the encounter will leave that customer dissatisfied. Dissatisfied customers are likely to tell others, take their business elsewhere, or stop doing business with you.

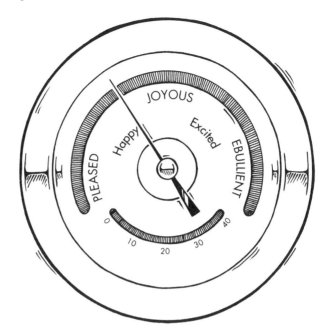

The key to success is to maintain happy customers. How is this done? By understanding customers' needs and by responding to those needs. Keep in mind that emotions are contagious. Look around you at the people you work with, those you serve, and those who serve you. What do you do when someone smiles at you? You smile back. What do you do when someone scowls at you? You probably don't smile back.

A Few Winning Ways

Humans are emotional beings, influenced by circumstances around them. With that in mind, think about your own emotions and how they factor into your customer interactions. If you can project an image of enthusiasm for your work, a degree of sensitivity for others, concern for the happiness and pleasure of your customers as you do business with then, you are very likely to win their loyalty. Put aside any sadness, anger, or fear you may be feeling when dealing with your customers and remember a few winning ways to make your customers feel good.

- Smile sincerely.
- Take a genuine interest in your customers and their needs.
- Treat your customers with respect.
- Put your customers at ease.

Now it's time to put what you have learned in this chapter into practice.

A couple seeks a restaurant for dinner before the premiere of a new musical. They run into traffic, have trouble finding a parking place, and end up in a very expensive parking garage next to the theater. Pressed for time, they hurry into the nearest restaurant, an intimate café that specializes in personal attention. A maitre d' greets them and shows them to a table by the window. A waitress appears to ask if they are interested in cocktails before dinner. When they ask for wine, she signals for the wine steward, who brings the wine list and leaves.

A busboy pours them water; the wine steward returns and begins the ritual of opening, sampling, and pouring the wine. Several moments pass before the waitress returns with the menu. She runs through the litany of today's specials, explaining the nuances of each dish's careful preparation. Orders in hand, she trots off to the kitchen and begins the process of a fine dining experience for the couple at table eight.

As the meal draws to a close, she begins to anticipate the tip the couple will leave. In her mind, she has offered them the special attention she was trained to provide, the hallmark that made the restaurant famous. She is pleased by her ability to pace the meal appropriately, allowing the couple to savor the salad and entrée before she approaches them to ask if they would care for dessert or coffee. But before she can wheel the dessert cart over, they signal for the check and leave moments later. When she clears the table after the couple's hasty departure, there is barely enough of a tip to cover the busboy, let alone herself or the wine steward.

The comment card left behind reveals another story. ''We were in a hurry to make an 8:00 P.M. curtain at the Savoy Theater. The waitress did everything she could to prolong the meal, sending over another waiter to take our drink order, dallying with our food, and virtually ignoring us after she brought the main course. We had to ask for the check. Thanks a lot for making us late.'' ■

Review & Practice

Answer the following questions.

1. What did the couple want from the encounter with the restaurant?

   _____

   _____

   _____

2. What factors influenced what the couple required from the experience?

   _____

   _____

   _____

3. What were the critical points of encounter for the couple?

   _____

   _____

   _____

4. What could the waitress have done to provide the service the customers expected?

   _____

   _____

   _____

5. What emotional state was the couple in when they completed the customer comment card?

   _____

   _____

   _____

Chapter Checkpoints

✓ Understand how needs affect behavior.

✓ Create positive customer encounters.

✓ Focus on the instances of impact.

✓ Remember that humans are emotional beings and emotions are contagious.

✓ Make your customers feel good.

3 | Uncovering Customer Needs

┌─── **This chapter will help you to:** ───────────────
│
│ ▪ Understand the importance of probing for customer needs.
│ ▪ Ask open-ended questions.
│ ▪ Recognize product/service features and benefits.
│ ▪ Understand tangible and intangible loss.
│
└───

Tanya Jones is walking through the showroom of a popular auto dealership. She stops to look at the sticker on a sleek, red, two-door sports car. David Chung, the salesman, approaches her.

"Would you like a new car?" he asks.

"Yes," Tanya responds.

"This one's a beauty," he begins. "Front-wheel drive, overhead cam engine. A real driving machine. Ever drive a five-speed?"

"Yes," Tanya answers.

"This one will do zero to 60 MPH in under a minute. Great suspension, too. Really hugs the curves. Steel-belted radials, leather interior, all the extras. Here," he says opening the door, "get behind the wheel and picture yourself driving this down the highway. Pretty comfortable, eh?"

"Mmmmm," Tanya sighs, getting out.

"Want to take one for a test drive?" David asks, expectantly.

"No, thanks," says Tanya, "the service department should have my van repaired soon. The guy who hit me was driving one of these. I don't think his car will be ready for weeks." ∎

WHY IS PROBING IMPORTANT?

In Chapter 2, you learned to identify what motivates customer behavior and the impact your own emotions play in responding positively to customer needs. Up to this point, the focus has been on looking at customers generically. To meet individual customer needs, you will need to master the art of probing. Probing requires the ability to concentrate on specific wants, desires, or problems customers are experiencing in order to present viable options to suit the specific situation.

Think about the last time you visited your doctor. If it was your first visit to the office, the receptionist handed you a form to fill out that asked a number of questions about your medical history and that of your family. Near the end, the form requested that you describe the reason for your visit. Before the doctor examined you, he or she reviewed the form with you, perhaps asking for additional information and making notes based on your responses.

Then the examination began, using instruments that allowed the doctor to look beyond the exterior to identify the source of the problem and to recommend a course of treatment. This proven technique of probing, along with years of technical training, allowed your doctor to prescribe a remedy for your problem or to offer some suggestions that would keep you in the best of health until your next visit.

The Art of Probing

Your customers will come to you with different needs and individual problems. You are responsible for uncovering those needs and solving problems so that you have happy, satisfied customers. By asking the right questions, you can determine what your customers want or need, and by paying careful attention to the answers, you can make educated recommendations to meet those needs. Learning to probe begins with formulating questions that elicit information from the customer to shed light on what the customer wants.

Open Versus Closed Questions

There are two basic types of questions: open and closed. Read and answer the following question:

Do you know what an open question is?

> Answer: _____

Most of you have probably written yes or no. With that question, that is all the information you are likely to provide. Quite simply, the question posed above is closed. A closed question usually elicits a response of yes or no and does not elicit any additional information. Closed questions limit discussion. Now answer this question.

What is an open question?

> Answer: _____

This time you have probably described what an open question is or have given an example that provides insight into your understanding of what an open question is. This second question is open—requiring more of an answer than yes or no. Generally, open questions start with who, what, how, why, when, which, tell me, or describe. The answers to open questions provide information and clues as to what the customer knows about your product or service, or what they need from it.

■ Review & Practice

Look at the following closed questions. Rewrite them in an open format.

> Closed: Do you currently have a checking account?
>
> Open: _____
>
> _____

> Closed: Have you used a VCR before?
>
> Open: _____
>
> _____

> Closed: Will you be needing a rental car?
>
> Open: _____
>
> _____

Closed: Is anyone traveling with you?

Open: _____

_____

Closed: May I help you?

Open: _____

_____

Closed: Have you been to our factory discount outlet?

Open: _____

_____

Closed: Is there a problem?

Open: _____

_____

There are a number of ways to rewrite closed questions in an open format. If you had any difficulty with the exercise, consider the following possible responses, then go back to the exercise and try it again.

Closed	Open
Do you currently have a checking account?	How do you currently pay your bills?
Have you used a VCR before?	Why are you considering buying a VCR?
Will you be needing a rental car?	How do you plan to get around the city after your arrival?
Is anyone traveling with you?	Who might be traveling with you?
May I help you?	How may I be of service to you today?
Have you been to our factory discount outlet?	When would you be available to visit our factory discount outlet?
Is there a problem?	Tell me exactly what trouble have you been experiencing?

Using open questions allows discussion to grow into a dialogue in which customers provide you with information about the purpose of their visit. If their purpose is to research your product or service before purchasing, you will be able to accommodate them by finding out how they plan to use the product or service and by making recommendations. If their purpose is to complain about service or quality, you will be able to identify the cause of the complaint and seek a solution.

Remember the following substitutions when changing a closed question to an open one:

Replace	With
Did you	When will you
Have you	Why have you
Is there	What is there
Do you	How do you
Will you	Tell me how you will
Can you	Describe how you can
Does someone	Who does
Was it	Which one was it

WHAT ARE THE FEATURES AND BENEFITS?

To provide quality service, the tools of the trade may not be as high-tech as the X rays and scanners your doctor uses to diagnose your physical health. In most industries, however, there are some practical methods to identify what the customer wants and to find out exactly what the customer needs to feel satisfied.

The Service Tool Kit

The first tool to have in your service tool kit is a comprehensive knowledge of the products and services your organization offers. Product knowledge goes a long way toward matching the right product or service to the customer's needs.

Features.   Start by studying your company's product or service manual. The manual should list specific items or groups of items in inventory, including price range and, ideally, features and benefits for each item. Features describe functions. They tell you and the customer exactly what the product does. An alarm clock has an on/off switch and mechanisms to set the time and to set the alarm. It may also offer a number of other features, such as a sleep timer, a snooze button, a brightness switch, a built-in radio, and a choice of sounds you may select to wake you up. These features describe the functions your alarm clock provides.

Benefits.   Benefits are ways the features enhance the value of the product or service to the individual. Let's look at the features of the alarm clock. A built-in radio allows the individual to select a favorite radio station to listen to or wake to and provides more than just a timepiece to the buyer. A sleep timer provides the flexibility of listening to the radio before falling asleep, but automatically shuts off after a predetermined interval so that the radio doesn't stay on all night. Very heavy sleepers may respond well to the option of waking to the sound of an insistent buzzer rather than a radio station. For those that wake frequently during the night and want to know what time it is, the switch that brightens the time display may be of importance. And a snooze bar allows the freedom of catching a few more minutes of sleep without the risk of oversleeping because the alarm will go off again in 5 or 10 minutes. These benefits are an interpretation of how the features meet the individual needs of the customer.

Hints ———————————————————————

Features *tell.*

Benefits *sell.*

Use the following chart to examine the features and benefits of your particular products or services.

Product/Service	Features	Benefits
_____	_____	_____
_____	_____	_____
_____	_____	_____
_____	_____	_____
_____	_____	_____
_____	_____	_____
_____	_____	_____
_____	_____	_____
_____	_____	_____
_____	_____	_____
_____	_____	_____
_____	_____	_____
_____	_____	_____
_____	_____	_____
_____	_____	_____
_____	_____	_____
_____	_____	_____
_____	_____	_____
_____	_____	_____
_____	_____	_____

Other Resources. Make sure you take the time to understand your products and services before you talk about features and benefits with your customers. Product brochures, promotional literature, and marketing bulletins can help. Talk with other employees and your manager. They can pinpoint questions customers are likely to ask or features that are particularly attractive. If your business requires demonstrating products, be sure you practice showing and operating the item, and try to anticipate benefits your customers may be seeking.

HOW DOES LOSS AFFECT YOUR CUSTOMERS?

The gap between satisfaction and dissatisfaction is often measured in loss. If a customer comes into your place of business with a set of expectations and those expectations are met and/or exceeded, that customer will walk away feeling satisfied. If the expectations are not met because needs have not been uncovered or, worse, uncovered but not matched with the appropriate product or service, the customer experiences a sense of loss. It is the perception of loss that often leads to complaints. There are two types of perceived loss: tangible and intangible.

Tangibles are the characteristics of a product or service that are concrete or real. For example, a customer walks into a fast-food restaurant to have lunch and purchases a hamburger, french fries, and a milk shake. The food items can be held, smelled, looked at, and tasted. They are the tangible qualities of the fast-food restaurant experience.

Intangibles arise from factors that are somewhat more elusive. In many cases, an intangible is simply an idea, a nonmaterial concept that accompanies the purchase of a product or service, but can rarely be measured. For example, it is implied that breath mints not only offer fresh breath but can actually bring you closer to others. Similarly, car dealers sell luxury cars by suggesting to the discerning buyer that a luxury automobile brings the owner increased status in the community. Both closeness and status are intangibles.

Customers expect both tangible and intangible satisfaction from the experience of doing business with you. A loss of either tangible or intangible satisfaction begins to unravel customer loyalty and trust.

Read the following situations and identify the tangible and intangible losses experienced by the customer.

Situation one: The bank where James Richardson has been doing business for the past 15 years is closing.
Tangible loss: _____

Intangible loss: _____

Situation two: Mary and Bill Somers go to the local movie theater to see the latest thriller. The film is sold out.
Tangible loss: _____

Intangible loss: _____

Situation three: Juanita Perez's brand-new car ends up in the repair shop three times in the first three months.
Tangible loss: _____

Intangible loss: _____

Situation four: The outfit Emma Nightingale orders by mail arrives in time for her dinner date, but the zipper is broken.
Tangible loss: _____

Intangible loss: _____

Although your responses may differ, consider the following possibilities.

Situation one

Tangible loss: James Richardson will have to get to know the staff at the new branch.

Intangible loss: The relationship of trust built over years has been broken for James Richardson.

Situation two

Tangible loss: Plans for an evening out will have to be adjusted because the theater is full.

Intangible loss: Mary and Bill Somers may be out of touch with friends who have already seen the film.

Situation three

Tangible loss: Juanita Perez will have to arrange substitute transportation and suffer the inconvenience.

Intangible loss: Juanita's trust in the car dealership is threatened, and she may begin to question her choice.

Situation four

Tangible loss: Emma Nightingale will have to find something else to wear and pay for the repair or return postage.

Intangible loss: Emma may begin to question the quality of other catalog items she may be interested in.

Pay attention to the tangible and intangible losses your customers may experience and look for ways to minimize these losses. In the following chapters, you will learn techniques for dealing with customers who perceive a sense of loss.

Review & Practice

Now it's time to put what you have learned in this chapter into practice.

You are a travel agent. Stephanie and Fred Lee, a working couple in their early 50s with a son and daughter in college, come into your office to plan their first trip without their children.

What questions will you ask them to determine what they want from their vacation?

1. _____

_____

_____

2. _____

_____

_____

3. _____

_____

_____

4. _____

_____

_____

5. _____

_____

_____

Based on the answers to your questions, you recommend an eight-day cruise to the Caribbean. You give them ship brochures that show smiling couples about their age lying by the pool, dining by candlelight, relaxing in elegant cabins, dancing in the moonlight, strolling on deserted beaches, and shopping at colorful markets on the islands.

What features does a Caribbean cruise offer and what are the benefits to the Lees?

Features: _____

_____

_____

_____

Benefits: _____

_____

_____

_____

Days before they are about to leave, the ship cancels the trip because of engine trouble. Deposits will be returned, but there is not enough time to book another trip for their planned vacation.

What are the tangible and intangible losses the Lees may experience as a result of their trip being canceled?

Tangible losses: _____

_____

_____

_____

Intangible losses: _____

_____

_____

_____

Chapter Checkpoints

✓ Probe to determine what your customers need.

✓ Ask open questions to get as much information as possible from your customers.

✓ Learn the features of your product or service.

✓ Talk about the benefits of your product or service with your customers.

✓ Appreciate the tangible and intangible losses your customers may experience and try to minimize them.

4 | Communication Is the Key

This chapter will help you to:

- Understand verbal and nonverbal messages.
- Use positive body language and voice tone.
- Use language your customers will understand.
- Actively listen to your customers.
- Communicate effectively over the telephone.

Max Dubovsky opens the door of the new fish market. It's Saturday and the store is very busy. The glass cases are well-lighted, clean, and filled with every imaginable kind of fish. One young man is arranging ice around buckets of steamers on display. People are pressed up against the glass examining the fresh catch and reading the signs. Behind the counter, several people are busy weighing and wrapping customers' selections. Max looks around to see if there is a number system for service. Finding none, he takes his place behind several other people. "Next," he hears and looks around to see who moves forward. "Over here," someone calls and the crowd surges to the left.

Max waits. The scene repeats itself several times, but Max still cannot determine who is in front of him. Finally, he catches the eye of the man behind the counter. "What'll it be?" he asks, checking his watch. "I'd like a pound of sea scallops," he asks.

"Whole or broken?"

"What's the difference?" he asks, looking at his recipe.

"About five dollars a pound." ∎

In Chapter 3, you learned the importance of probing customers to determine their needs. You also learned how to phrase questions that elicit pertinent information and to focus your attention on describing product and service benefits based on customer needs. Finally, you looked at tangible and intangible loss. Understanding how loss affects the customer's perception of value is an important building block in learning how to provide quality when servicing your customers. In this chapter, you will take a closer look at how you can use communication techniques to prepare, present, and polish your customer service skills.

WHAT ARE VERBAL AND NONVERBAL MESSAGES?

Communication involves both mind and body. Most people think of communication as words and language. But language is only a small part of total communication. Several other factors affect the meaning of your message. Gestures, facial expressions, and voice tone and inflection can change the intended meaning of the message. As a result, customers may not always hear and understand what you intend for them to hear and understand. By paying attention to both verbal and nonverbal messages, you can positively shape communication with your customers.

Verbal Communication

Oral, or verbal, communication is more than just spoken words. Most important is not so much what you say as how you say it. Experts agree that only 20 percent of your message is communicated face-to-face through words; 45 percent is communicated by the quality of your voice tone and inflection. The rest of your message is transmitted through body language, or nonverbal communication.

Nonverbal Communication

Body language is an intriguing topic that has fascinated researchers for years. Who has not passed time waiting in airports or sitting in doctors' offices watching people? When people are unaware of others watching them, they are more relaxed and revealing. Look around you through your day, and observe the way people sit or stand, how they use their hands, and the expressions on their faces. Each facet of an individual's body language is a clue to what he or she is thinking or feeling and may contrast directly with what is being said.

Read the following descriptions of gestures, positions, or facial expressions, and write down what you think each communicates.

1. Arms crossed: _____
2. Chin resting in hand: _____
3. Tapping fingers on table: _____
4. Pacing: _____
5. Furrowed brow: _____
6. Leaning back in chair: _____
7. Shaking head from side to side: _____
8. Rolling the eyes: _____
9. Nodding head up and down: _____
10. Shrugging shoulders: _____

Although there are many interpretations of such body language, some broad universal meanings are presented here for your consideration.

1. Close-minded, unwilling to listen.
2. Bored, tired, or disinterested.
3. Impatient, bored.
4. Nervous, tense.
5. Thoughtful, concerned.
6. Comfortable, casual, or relaxed.
7. Disbelieving, distrustful.
8. Skeptical, sarcastic.
9. In agreement, encouraging.
10. Uncommitted, unknowing.

READ BETWEEN THE LINES

No matter how you interpret the meaning of body language, it is clear that messages are being communicated through more than words. Keep this in mind when working with your customers. You will need to "read between the lines" of what your customers are saying and, more importantly, use your own body language to communicate concern, interest, and understanding.

Positive Posturing

"Shoulders back, head up, stomach in." The admonitions your parents and teachers made when you were younger still go a long way in creating a positive impression. Presenting a professional image makes a lasting impact on customers. Being well-groomed is important in any business,

Positive Postures	Negative Postures
Smiling.	Frowning.
Solid handshake.	Weak, limp handshake.
Sitting up straight.	Slouching.
Relaxed, open arms.	Arms crossed or hands in pockets.
Maintaining eye contact.	
Leaning forward to listen closely.	Looking up, down, or away from the customer.
Nodding head in acknowledgment or encouragement.	Tapping fingers.
	Frequent glancing at clock.

but when working with customers it is critical. Consider your reaction to the waiter who is slovenly dressed, unkempt, or dirty. How would his appearance affect your dining experience?

Positive postures reflect interest in and concern for the customer. Practice positive postures in the mirror or ask a friend to help you. The reward will be worth it.

Voice Tone

The way you speak is also important. Voice tone and inflection can change the meaning of your words. Attitudes are expressed in voice tone. Conversations that start out pleasantly can become difficult if one of the speakers becomes tense or upset. Try reading the following sentence in a voice that expresses a different attitude each time. Use a tape recorder so that you can listen to the changes in your voice tone.

"How may I help you today?"

- Angry.
- Annoyed.
- Concerned.
- Confident.
- Helpful.
- Tense.
- Upset.

Inflection and Pitch

Note that the message, "how may I help you today" changes its meaning each time you read it with a new attitude. Inflection can also change the message. Inflection refers to emphasizing certain words to make them stand out. Sometimes by putting the emphasis at the end of a sentence, the whole meaning of the sentence can change from a statement to a question. This happens when the pitch, or level, of your voice goes from low to high. Try reading the following sentences emphasizing the word in bold each time. Record and listen to how inflection can change the meaning.

"**Thank** you for calling and please come again."

"Thank you for **calling** and please come again."

"Thank **you** for calling and please come again."

"Thank you for calling and **please** come again."

"Thank you for calling and please come **again**."

Understanding how voice tone and inflection changes the meaning of words can help you choose the most positive way to communicate your messages.

CHOOSING THE RIGHT WORDS

Word choice can make a difference. The English language is comprised of hundreds of thousands of words. Several words can be used to convey the same or a similar message. List, for example, as many words as you think of that mean the same thing as the word customer.

_____	_____
_____	_____
_____	_____
_____	_____

The list could probably be a lot longer, but you probably came up with some of the following: buyer, shopper, bargain-hunter, consumer, client, user, end user, patron, purchaser, bill payer, subscriber.

Keep it Simple

The exercise illustrates the subtle differences in language. Those differences can mean a great deal. How would your customers react to being called a bill payer or a user? A good rule of thumb is to keep the language you use with customers simple, clear, positive, and enthusiastic. Avoid jargon, technical terms, and abbreviations at all costs. Jargon, language used inside an organization or industry, is senseless to the public. Technical terms and abbreviations can be confusing. For example, the banking industry has CSRs, or customer service representatives, and the travel industry has CRSs, or computer reservation systems. These nonsensical terms have no meaning to your customers, and it is best to avoid using them.

Accentuate the Positive

Words should convey the positive and avoid the negative. Think before you speak. Take responsibility for your customers and offer them choices. How would you feel if, after waiting in line to return a broken wiper blade, you were told: "You'll have to take that to the automotive department," or: "That's not my department."

Rephrase the following negative statements with responses that accentuate the positive, demonstrate taking responsibility, or offer choices.

Negative: You're in the wrong department.
Positive: _____
_____

Negative: We don't carry those.
Positive: _____
_____

Negative: It's company policy.
Positive: _____
_____

Negative: I don't know.
Positive: _____
_____

Negative: You forgot to sign it.
Positive: _____
_____

Negative: You'll have to show some ID.
Positive: _____
_____

Positive Substitutes.   Turning negative statements into positive comments is a skill you can learn to master with a little practice. Read the following suggestions if you had any trouble with the previous exercise; then practice making up your own substitutes.

Negative: You're in the wrong department.
Positive: Let me show you where we keep those. They're in the cosmetics department for future reference.

Negative: We don't carry those.
Positive: I'd be glad to see if we could order that item for you.

Negative: It's company policy.
Positive: For your protection, we ask for complete payment within 24 hours.

Negative: I don't know.
Positive: Let me find someone who can answer that for you.

Negative: You forgot to sign it.
Positive: You've completed the form correctly. If you'll just sign here, I can place the order for you.

Negative: You'll have to show some ID.
Positive: May I see your driver's license please?

More Positive Phrases.   Try using the following phrases to convey a positive attitude to your customers.

- Certainly! I'd be glad to . . . .
- What may I assist you with?
- Call me if you need further assistance.
- I appreciate your patience.
- Thank you for your inquiry.
- What would you prefer? The options would be . . . .
- Thank you for the suggestion.
- You made a good choice.
- May I place you on hold while I find the information?

WHAT IS ACTIVE LISTENING?

You learned in previous chapters that customers expect to be pleased with their purchases, to enjoy the encounter with your place of business, and to feel good about themselves when their interaction with you is over. A number of interpersonal skills are involved in meeting these expectations, but one of the most important is showing an interest in your customers. Whether they walk into your store, sit down at your desk, or call you on the telephone, customers want to feel that they are important to you at that time. You can make customers feel that way by actively listening to what they have to say. Active listening means becoming involved in the conversation, demonstrating interest, and paying attention to verbal and nonverbal messages.

Showing Interest

Recall a recent conversation with someone who demonstrated a genuine interest in what you were saying. Describe the situation in as much detail as possible. Focus on what the other person said or did to make you feel that he or she was listening to you.

What did the other person do (facial expressions, gestures, body posture) to indicate interest? _____

_____

_____

_____

_____

What did the other person say (questions or comments) to indicate interest? _____

_____

_____

_____

_____

Your answer to the first question most likely referred to such things as maintaining eye contact, smiling, nodding in agreement or acknowledgment, leaning forward, taking notes, or being in close proximity to you as you were speaking.

Your answer to the second question may have included phrases such as "I see what you mean," "yes, I agree," "that's true," or some other comment that indicated the other party was listening. Other possibilities include being asked questions to clarify what you meant to make sure they understood.

A third question could have been added to the exercise asking what the other person did *not* do that indicated interest. Overwhelmingly, the answer would have been: "He (or she) did not interrupt me."

The Research Is In.   Researchers have found that a person can comprehend 500 words per minute; however, most people speak at an average rate of between 125 and 155 words per minute. This means that the average listener need only pay attention 25 percent of the time, leaving plenty of room for distractions that affect the quality of listening. How often have you found yourself daydreaming or mentally composing your response while your customer is still speaking?

What This Means for You.

What does this mean for service providers? Quite simply, that taking a genuine interest in your customers requires that you take an active role. It does not mean that you monopolize the conversation or overpower your customers with words. You can demonstrate your interest in what they have to say with a few very simple techniques that will keep you actively involved in the conversation.

Active Listening Techniques
- Maintain eye contact.
- Smile.
- Don't interrupt.
- Nod in acknowledgment.
- Repeat important points.
- Probe for additional information.
- Take notes.

WHAT ABOUT THE TELEPHONE?

So far, this chapter has focused primarily on face-to-face contact with your customers. But some of your customer encounters will take place over the telephone. Many of the service techniques discussed apply to telephone communication as well. It is critical to project the best professional image through your voice because messages delivered over the telephone rely 90 percent on voice and only 10 percent on actual words.

4

Call Your Competitors

Try calling some of your competitors to inquire about their products and services over the telephone. Prepare your questions in advance and listen to their responses as well as how they are delivered. After you complete the conversations, answer the following questions.

1. What was the person's name? Did you have to ask for it, or did you have to ask him or her to repeat the name?

_____

_____

_____

2. What do you think the person looked like, based on the image he or she projected over the telephone?

_____

_____

_____

3. What voice qualities did the person use to give you this image?

_____

_____

_____

4. What do you think the person was doing while talking with you?

_____

_____

_____

5. What information did the other person learn from you during the conversation?

_____

_____

_____

6. What information did you learn from the other person during the conversation?

_____

_____

_____

You may have had surprising results depending on how many calls you made. Learn from your own experience with the telephone survey above. No doubt you formed some strong impressions about the quality of service from spending a few minutes talking with your competitors.

All you have to go on in forming an impression over the telephone is the quality of the voice. Use the telephone to your advantage by practicing a few basic principles of telephone communication.

Articulate Clearly.   Because the telephone distorts the sound of your voice, it is necessary to articulate your words clearly. Practice saying, "Good morning. Miss Star." If rushed or mumbled, this could easily sound like, "Good morning, mister." Try to speak slowly with enough volume that the caller can understand you. Chewing gum, drinking coffee, or smoking cigarettes also will affect your ability to articulate clearly.

Use the Customer's Name.   Ask for and use the name of the caller. Customers want to be treated as individuals; using their names personalizes the conversation.

Project Confidence.   Use your voice tone to instill a sense of confidence in the customer. Speaking in a monotone sounds mechanical, forced, and rehearsed. By varying your voice pitch, you can convey interest and enthusiasm.

Respond Visually.   With each telephone conversation, try to visualize the caller. Put an imaginary face to the voice at the other end of the line. This will help you respond to an individual rather than an anonymous voice. Even though callers cannot see you, they can hear a great deal in your voice. Smile while speaking—they will hear the smile. Facial expressions automatically change the quality of your voice and help to convey interest in the customer. Use your own personality to animate your conversations.

Eliminate Distractions.   It is not impossible to do two things at once, but it is difficult. Turn down the radio, stop using your computer or typewriter, and don't try to carry on another conversation while you are on the telephone. Your customers expect and deserve your complete attention.

It Takes Two

At least two people are involved in any telephone conversation. If you seem to be doing all the talking, pause to let the customer ask questions or add information. If the customer is doing most of the talking, show that you are listening by asking clarifying questions or injecting "I see," or "Yes, I understand," when appropriate.

Tape some of your telephone conversations and listen to the sound of your own voice. Use the following feedback form to rate yourself. Circle 1 if you need some work in this area; circle 5 if you're satisfied with the way you sound. Do periodic checks of your telephone voice to stay in top form.

MY TELEPHONE VOICE

Volume	1	2	3	4	5
Articulation	1	2	3	4	5
Pitch	1	2	3	4	5
Attitude	1	2	3	4	5
Animation	1	2	3	4	5

◼ Review & Practice

Sumitro and Ann Leman walk into Prospective Properties to talk to a realtor about buying a house. Andrew Wolske, a realtor, is on the phone.

"Well, Mrs. Jones," he shouts into the receiver, "they made some changes to the P and S. The wordage is different in one of the contingency clauses, and we'll have to add a rider." He leans back in the chair, tucks his feet up under him, lights a cigarette, and motions to the young couple to come in and sit down. "How d'ya make out at the bank?" he continues. He cups his hand over the mouthpiece and whispers, "She's deaf," and rolls his eyes. "What do you young kids need?" "No, no, no!" he yells back on the phone, "with 20 down you don't need PMI."

Sumitro shows Andrew the ad circled in the newspaper. "Oh, that's a great little fixer-upper. Hang on and let me get you the specs," Andrew says as he reaches for the files behind him. The receiver slips from his shoulder and falls to the floor. "Oops," he chuckles and shrugs his shoulders. "Listen, Mrs. Jones. I can't help you. Talk to your banker and call me when it's firm."

"So," Andrew turns to Sumitro and Ann, getting out the listings, "ready for a place of your own, are you?" ■

1. What impression do you think Andrew made on Sumitro and Ann?

_____

_____

_____

_____

2. Describe Andrew's body language. What may it have communicated to Sumitro and Ann? _____

_____

_____

_____

3. Did Andrew demonstrate an interest in his conversation with Mrs. Jones? Why or why not? If not, what could he have said or done to show his interest? _____

_____

_____

_____

4. How could Andrew have dealt more effectively with having a customer on the telephone and two more waiting in his office?

_____

_____

_____

_____

Chapter Checkpoints

✓ Understand the impact of verbal and nonverbal messages.

✓ Use voice tone, inflection, and positive body language when communicating with your customers.

✓ Choose words that your customers will understand.

✓ Listen actively by demonstrating interest in your customers.

✓ Project your best self over the phone—customers respond to *how* you deliver a message even more than *what* you actually say.

5 | A Five-Star Approach to Problem Resolution

This chapter will help you to:

- Acknowledge customer problems.
- Assess the circumstances of the problem.
- Affirm your understanding of the problem.
- Analyze alternative solutions.
- Agree on a plan to solve the problem.

Cindy Ferguson waits patiently at the customer service desk to return the wedding gift she received from her aunt.

"Next in line," says one of the salespeople without looking up.

Cindy puts the box on the counter. "I'd like to return this can opener . . ." she starts.

"Do you have a receipt?" asks the salesperson, who is completing the previous transaction.

"No, it was a gift," explains Cindy.

"No returns without a receipt, ma'am. Company policy," replies the salesperson, still writing.

"It was a wedding gift from my aunt in California. I don't have a receipt. I'd just like to . . . ." Cindy tries again.

"Sorry, ma'am. I can't take it without a receipt." She points to the sign behind her. "See, company policy. With a receipt, no problem. Without a receipt, I can't help you. Next."

"But I told you it was a gift and I don't have a receipt," Cindy exclaims, her voice rising. "And I don't need two can openers. What am I supposed to do?" ∎

The first four chapters of this book prepared you for your role in providing customer service. You learned about your responsibilities to customers and their expectations; the importance of understanding customer needs and the skills to uncover them; and effective communication techniques in building a relationship between you and your customers. Now it is time to look at the thorny issue of customer problems—how to recognize them and what to do about them when they occur.

In this chapter, you will learn how to use five simple steps to address any customer problem. Some problems that you encounter will be easier to solve than others. If you apply the five basic rules of problem resolution, not only will you find a solution, but you will likely retain the customer's loyalty and minimize criticism the customer may have about the quality of your product or service. We will address each step of this five-star approach.

The Five-Star Approach
- Acknowledge the customer.
- Assess the situation.

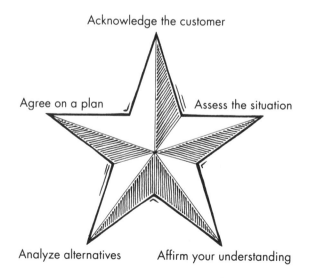

- Affirm your understanding.
- Analyze alternatives.
- Agree on a plan.

Acknowledge
the customer

ACKNOWLEDGE THE CUSTOMER

The first step is to acknowledge the customer. Start by greeting the customer and indicating your availability to help. The greeting is an established approach to each new customer that calls or enters your business. Some businesses have standardized greetings such as "Good morning. How may I help you today?" If your business requires a standard greeting, try to make it sound fresh and new each time you say it by modulating your voice tone, inflection, and pitch. If your greeting is not standardized, select words of welcome that reflect your enthusiasm and interest in serving the customer.

In the space below, list some possible greetings for your business.

1. _____
2. _____
3. _____
4. _____
5. _____

Customer Responses

Your greeting will elicit from the customer a response that indicates what they need. In a problem situation, customers can respond in a number of different ways. Some may calmly describe the problem and ask for your help. Others may be accusatory, as if the problem was all your fault. Still others may be angry or defiant, making demands of you and the company you represent. Remember to watch their body language and listen to the tone of their voices. This will give you a clue to their emotional state, which will help you determine how to deal with them.

Opening Lines of Communication

Once the customer makes it clear that there is problem, you must acknowledge the problem. Acknowledging that the customer has a problem does not necessarily mean that you understand what the problem is or that you have a plan to solve it. It merely means that you recognize that the customer has encountered some aspect of the product or service that is causing displeasure. By recognizing that a problem exists, you will help to diffuse any anger or hostility the customer may be feeling. Practice writing opening lines to the following problem statements.

1. Problem: "I've been in the checkout line for over 20 minutes. Where are all the cashiers?"

Response: _____

_____

_____

2. Problem: "I paid for this item last month. Why is it still on my bill?"

Response: _____

_____

_____

3. Problem: "This is not what I ordered. When will you people get it right?"

Response: _____

_____

_____

4. Problem: "I've called three times today and no one has returned my call."

Response: _____

_____

_____

5. Problem: "You promised me it would be delivered today. Where is it?"

Response: _____

_____

_____

Suggested Responses.   Remember, at this point, you have just become aware that the customer has a problem. Before you go any further, you want to acknowledge how they are feeling and show them that you want to help. The best response will be short and simple.

1. "I'm sorry you have had such a long wait. Let me see what I can do."
2. "That's a good question. I can look into that for you."
3. "We made a mistake. Let me see if what you want is in stock."

4. "I can understand why you would be upset. Let me help you."

5. "I'm sorry you have not received it yet. Let me look into why it's been delayed."

ASSESS THE SITUATION

Now you and the customer are aware a problem exists. The next step is to assess the situation. Use your probing skills to get as much information from the customer as you need to understand the circumstances. As you seek information, demonstrate your interest in the customer's situation with active listening. Take notes, maintain eye contact during face-to-face encounters, and use your communication skills to effectively determine the nature of the problem.

Some Pitfalls

It is important to phrase questions carefully when assessing the nature of the problem. At this point, the customer may be very emotional—annoyed, angry, frustrated. You want to avoid upsetting the customer any further. You are not looking for excuses and should not offer them; you do not want to place blame on the customer or on your company or its employees. Think of yourself as a detective or fact-finder. Ask questions that will provide answers to what happened, not why it happened or who did it. Give the customer an opportunity to explain the details that will help you find a solution.

Practice Assessing

Read the following customer situation.

Elena Manrara brought in her computer to be repaired last week. She was promised it would be ready today at noon. When she arrived at 12:30 P.M. it still wasn't ready. Finally, after she waited 45 minutes, her computer was returned. When she got home, she plugged it in and turned it on. Now she is on the telephone telling you that she received shoddy service because her computer is still broken.

What questions will you ask Elena to help you understand the problem?

1. _____

2. _____

3. _____

4. _____

Fact-Finding Questions.   Finding the facts is best accomplished by asking open questions. In Elena's situation, you need to know what's wrong with the computer. Some possible questions you might ask to assess this situation include:

1. Describe what happened when you turned on the computer.
2. What was the reason you brought the computer to the shop?
3. What did the service person tell you was done to the computer?
4. What other problems have you had with the computer in the past?

Hidden Issues.   The answers Elena provides to these questions will begin to give you an idea of what might be wrong with the computer. Elena also may be upset about the wait in the shop or that you (the computer repair shop) broke your promise to her (to have the computer ready at noon). These are actually two hidden issues. Elena may tell you about the delay in service or she may focus only on the computer repair itself. Two additional questions might help you to understand her comment about shoddy service.

1. Were there any other problems with our service that I should know about?
2. How were you informed that the computer was ready?

By demonstrating your interest in providing quality service to her, this questioning could open the door for Elena to tell you about the expectations she had in doing business with your company and may help to diffuse any anger or hostility she is feeling.

AFFIRM YOUR UNDERSTANDING

Affirm your
understanding

Now that you have assessed the circumstances involved in the situation, it is time to affirm what you have learned with the customer. This step allows the customer to confirm what you know and add additional information if needed. By affirming your understanding, you will again diffuse any negative emotions the customer may be feeling. In this step, you begin to form a partnership with the customer that will be crucial later in finding alternative solutions.

Provide Assurance

The customer has now had an opportunity to explain the problem to you. You need to provide some assurance that you not only heard what was said but that you understand the problem and plan to act on it. Paraphrase, or repeat, what the customer told you and indicate that you are willing to check into it. For example, "So Mr. Smith, you expected your car to be ready by 4:00 P.M. and the repairs aren't finished. Let me find out what's taking so long." The customer will appreciate knowing that someone listened to and understood the problem.

Practice Paraphrasing

Read the following customer accounts of problem situations, and pick out the key words or phrases that you would paraphrase to indicate your understanding of the situation.

Customer: "I just got a notice in the mail that one of my checks bounced and now I have to pay a $20 fee. I deposited my paycheck last Friday. Why didn't you credit my account? I've never been so humiliated."

Key words/phrases: _____

_____

_____

Customer: "I called two days ago to make reservations for dinner tonight. I'm entertaining an important client and I asked for the best table in the house. We're sitting next to the kitchen. You call that the best table in the house?"

Key words/phrases: _____

_____

_____

Customer: "That shipment was supposed to be delivered last week. Now we're behind schedule and I have to tell my client his order will be late. What kind of business are you running here?"

Key words/phrases: _____

_____

_____

Customer: "Who does the accounting around here? This is the second time in two months I've been overcharged. I want to speak to the manager."

Key words/phrases: _____

_____

_____

Empathize with Your Customers

Empathy is the ability to understand how a person feels without sharing or displaying the same feeling. Customers want to know that you appreciate them and their business. Let them know that you are willing to listen and that you are empathetic. When customers experience a problem with your products or services, make an effort to assure them that you understand and plan to take action.

Analyze
alternatives

ANALYZE ALTERNATIVES

After both you and the customer understand the problem and all the factors involved, the real work begins. Now it is time to begin putting together a plan that will meet the customer's needs without compromising the relationship any further. In most situations, there are several different approaches to solving the problem. Since not all of the possible solutions will meet with the customer's satisfaction, you and the customer must analyze the alternatives and find the best possible solution together.

Form a Team

You and the customer now share the problem. He or she has come to you with a difficult situation and you have listened and demonstrated your understanding of the circumstances. Now you are a team; the problem is yours together. To reach the best possible solution, you must build on your partnership.

Brainstorm Solutions

The best way to solve any problem is to generate ideas that will meet the present need and avoid repeating the problem in the future. If you involve the customer in the decision-making process, the likelihood increases that the plan will be accepted. Ask the customer what can be done to solve the present situation. Brainstorm options that will bring the situation to a positive end. Neither of you are committing to an answer yet. You are generating a list of possible solutions that will have to be evaluated to determine if they will work.

Compromise

Generating a list of solutions makes the situation more manageable. What originally looked like a problem now has one or more possible solutions. Often it is only a matter of looking at each solution to find one that works for both parties involved. This method often ends in compromise, where each party loses a little and gains a great deal. Take a look at the following example.

Paul Linder goes to his closet to take out the hand-knit sweater he recently had cleaned to wear on his date tonight. As he takes the garment out of the plastic bag, he notices two small holes in the front of the sweater that weren't there when he brought it to the dry cleaner. He carefully examines the entire sweater to see if there has been any other damage. To his horror, he notices that five of the eight buttons are chipped or melted and discovers a dye stain on the back. He is furious. The next morning, he returns to the dry cleaner with sweater in hand. Patiently, he shows the employee the damage done to his sweater. The employee empathizes with Paul, explains what might have happened, and asks him what he would like to do about the situation. ■

Solution 1: Paul suggests that the dry cleaner refund the cost of the original dry cleaning expenses and reimburse him for the sweater.

Solution 2: The dry cleaner offers to mend the holes, replace the buttons, and try to remove the stain.

What are the gains and losses for Paul and the dry cleaner with each solution? Fill in the charts below.

Solution 1	Paul	Dry cleaner
Gains		
Losses		

Solution 2	Paul	Dry cleaner
Gains		
Losses		

Sample Answer

Solution 1	Paul	Dry cleaner
Gains	Refund of drycleaning costs. Price of a new sweater.	Confidence of customer.
Losses	Original sweater	Money for refund. Cost of new sweater.

Solution 2	Paul	Dry cleaner
Gains	Keeps the original sweater. Saves cost of repairs.	Confidence of customer.
Losses	Use of sweater while being repaired.	Cost of repairs.

Agree on a plan

AGREE ON A PLAN

You and the customer have reviewed the possible alternatives and discussed the pros and cons of each. Some solutions may require further research or data-gathering. You may have to check with your manager to obtain authority to waive fees, to find out if an item is in stock, or to check the delivery schedule in the shipping department. Before you commit to a plan, make sure you can deliver what you promise.

Gain Commitment

Once you have assured the customer that you will take action to correct the problem, you need to gain the customer's commitment to a plan of action. Ask the customer if he or she will agree to the plan. For example, "I'll call the other stores to see if any of them have that item in stock and call you by 3:00 P.M. today. Would that be okay with you?" Once you have gained commitment, you will work toward bringing the situation to a positive end, keeping the customer informed of your progress. Always follow up to prevent further dissatisfaction that might arise.

Unresolved Issues

5

There may be times when you will not be able to resolve problems no matter how well you use the five-star approach. Your customers may be too emotional to cooperate, or the action needed may exceed your authority or area of responsibility. In some cases, the problem crosses several areas of responsibility of which you might be only one part. Don't give up. You can take one last step to begin the problem resolution process. Refer the problem to your manager for assistance; customers often respond differently when the manager gets involved. This step also works well with customers that get violent or threaten you. Immediately seek assistance to avoid an abusive situation.

Review & Practice

Write your own customer scenario based on a real experience you had with a customer who brought a problem to your attention. Briefly describe the details of the situation in the space provided below.

_____

_____

_____

_____

_____

_____

_____

_____

_____

Use the five-star approach to resolve the customer's problem. Write how you would respond now, having read this chapter.

1. How would you acknowledge the problem?

_____

_____

_____

2. What questions would you ask to assess the situation?

_____

_____

_____

3. What would you say to affirm your understanding of the problem?

_____

_____

_____

4. What are alternative solutions to this problem?

_____

_____

_____

5. Choose one of the possible solutions to the problem. What steps need to be taken to put the plan into action? What time frames will you impose on each step? When will you follow up with the customer?

_____

_____

_____

Chapter Checkpoints

✓ Acknowledge problems that customers bring to your attention.

✓ Seek information and ask questions that clarify the situation.

✓ Let the customer know you understand the problem.

✓ Look for alternative solutions to the problem with your customer.

✓ Agree on a plan of action, and always follow up with the customer.

6 | Lasting Impressions

> **This chapter will help you to:**
> - Close customer encounters effectively.
> - Say no with positive results.
> - Deal with stress.

Ronald Boros dialed the number of the ticket outlet. "Hello. Half-Price Ticket Outlet. All representatives are currently busy. Please hold," he heard. Ronald waited for nearly 10 minutes. Finally, a representative came on the line.

"This is Robin. May I help you?" she said.

"Yes. I'd like tickets to Saturday's performance at the Baron Theater."

"I'm sorry. We don't have any tickets for that performance."

"What about Sunday?"

"No, sorry."

"Friday?" he tried.

"No," came the reply.

"Well," he said, feeling exasperated, "do you have any tickets at all?"

"No, sir. That show has been sold out for weeks."

"Well, then why are you still advertising it in the paper!" he shouted into the phone. "Do you enjoy wasting people's time?"

"Sir, I don't print the ads," Robin countered. "Have a nice day," she told him, disconnecting the call.

"You know," she said to the representative next to her, "these people are starting to give me a headache. Is it my fault they wait until the last minute?" ■

HOW DO YOU EFFECTIVELY CLOSE CUSTOMER ENCOUNTERS?

Bringing customer encounters to an effective close is as important as the greeting in creating a lasting impression that will keep customers coming back. The time you have spent building the relationship, establishing rapport, and probing for needs is critical, but the last few minutes can undo all the good work you have done if the customer leaves feeling dissatisfied or unappreciated. Closings provide an opportunity to ensure that you have met the customer's needs. Now is the time to ask how else you can be of service and remind your customers that you value their business.

In Person

If the customer visited you at the store or office, you have the advantage of communicating your sincerity through body language and eye contact. The words you choose to deliver your final message should be reflected by the tone of your voice and your body posture. The principles of effective communication can be applied whatever the result of the encounter—whether the customer was comparison shopping, asking for information, making a purchase, or complaining. Follow these tips when closing an encounter:

- Ask if there is anything else you can do for them.
- Smile sincerely.
- Stand, if the customer is standing.
- Shake the customer's hand.
- Offer your business card, if you have one.

- Invite them to call or visit if they have questions or concerns.
- Use the customer's name, if you know it.
- Make an appropriate personal comment, or compliment them on their purchase, if they made one ("I know you are going to enjoy your new car," or "Congratulations on your new house").
- Thank the customer for coming in.

Over the Telephone

The same strategy applies to telephone encounters, with slight modifications due to the lack of visual contact. On the telephone, your voice tone and inflection are the keys to conveying your message with sincerity. Let the customer hear the smile in your voice and the warmth in your tone. Repeat your business telephone number instead of offering your business card, and invite the customer to call again if he or she needs further information or has questions. Remind customers of your business hours to ensure that they will receive personal service. Always thank the customer for calling.

Practice Your Closings

Your closing should be as genuine as your greeting. If your place of business has a standard closing, make it sound fresh by modulating voice tone and inflection. Even the old standby "Have a nice day" can sound special if delivered with enthusiasm. Practice writing customer closings in the space below. Remember to treat your customers as individuals. Listen to what they say during your encounter so that you can personalize the closing when it is time.

In-person closing: _____

_____

_____

Telephone closing: _____

_____

_____

WHAT IF THE ANSWER IS NO?

You have listened to the customer, demonstrated your concern for him or her, used strategies to find the facts and analyze the situation, but you find that you are unable to offer help. You have to say no—it is not possible to correct the problem, the item is out of stock, your tables are full, or the request is unreasonable. No matter how you look at it or how much you want to say yes, the answer is no and you must tell the customer. How do you say no without losing the customer forever? The answer lies in how you deliver the message.

Your Own Story

Recall a recent occasion when you had to say no to a customer. Briefly describe the circumstances of the situation, giving the details of the request and the factors behind why you had to say no.

_____
_____
_____
_____
_____
_____
_____
_____
_____

Refer to this situation as you read about techniques for saying no.

Use the Facts

Suppose that as you work with a customer to find possible solutions to his or her problem, you encounter stumbling blocks that prevent the plan from meeting the customer's needs, or you find that the customer's request is beyond what you or your company can deliver. If, for example, the customer has asked for the leather boots you are showing her in red and you know that the manufacturer does not make them in red, you will have to tell her that the boots do not come in red. You can temper the news with a brief apology and them simply tell the customer, "I'm sorry. These boots do not come in red." It's hard to argue with the truth.

Be Firm, but Gentle

When a customer requests something you cannot provide, the best way to handle the situation is firmly, but gently. Make sure that the customer does not feel personally rejected.

Imagine for a moment that you are the maitre d' of a small, popular restaurant. It is Saturday night, all the tables are full, and a large party has reserved a corner of the restaurant for a private party. Your regular customers, Leslie and David Vega, come in without a reservation. They ask for a table and you have none to give them. You do not want to offend them or lose their patronage in the future. However, you must tell them that tonight you just do not have a table for them. You might say, "I wish I'd known you were going to come in tonight. It's always nice to see you. But, as you can see, we're completely booked."

This response gently tells the Vegas that you appreciate their business, but dinner in your restaurant tonight is out of the question. Suggest another way to say no to the Vegas that is both gentle and firm.

_____

_____

Remain Calm

Some customers just won't take no for an answer. They may continue to insist that you meet their needs even though you have already told them that you cannot. One strategy to use in this situation is to remain calm and repeat your message until the customer eventually hears what you are saying and moves on. You will need to maintain control so that your voice will not betray any feeling of impatience or frustration. Consider the customer who insists on a four-door rental car when all you have left on the lot are two-door models.

"I want a four-door sedan."

"I'm sorry. The only cars we have left have two doors."

"But I requested a four-door."

"I can let you have any of the two-door models you see on the lot."

"I want a four-door."

"There are plenty of two-door models available."

If you continue to state the situation politely and matter-of-factly, the customer will eventually relent or move on.

Provide Reasons, Not Excuses

Customers usually respond positively when they understand the reason you are unable to meet their request. Provide them with reasons, not excuses, that prevent you from meeting their needs. It's easy to hide behind an excuse, such as "It's company policy." That means nothing to the customer. Turn the excuse into a reason the customer can understand. "Our identification policy allows us to ensure that funds are distributed to the rightful owner."

Offer Alternatives

Wherever possible, when telling a customer no, offer an alternative. Customers will hear yes if you offer them something that you can do for them when you tell them no. Read the two statements below. Which one sounds more positive to you?

"We don't carry that model."

"We don't have that model, but we do carry a similar model with all the features of the one you want at an attractive price."

By offering alternatives, you provide customers with an opportunity to consider other options that may not have occurred to them. Your effort demonstrates that you value their business and are willing to help. This strategy can turn a loss into a gain for you and the customer.

Rewrite the following statements to offer alternatives to the customer.

"We don't carry that dress in your size."
Rewrite: _____
_____
_____

"That flight has been canceled."
Rewrite: _____
_____
_____

"The item you ordered is out of stock."
Rewrite: _____
_____
_____

"We don't accept personal checks."
Rewrite: _____
_____
_____

"We don't deliver."

Rewrite: _____

_____

_____

End Politely

When you have tried all the strategies for saying no and the customer is still angry and dissatisfied, end politely. Thank the customer for bringing the situation to your attention. At the very least, you have become aware of a customer service area that needs attention. Remember, customers that have problems and don't let you know about them are the ones to fear. They simply walk away and take their business elsewhere.

WHAT CAN YOU DO ABOUT STRESS?

Certainly, dealing with customers can be stressful. You encounter a variety of customers with different wants, needs, and desires. You are responsible to meet those needs and provide the best possible service at all times. Some customers have requests that you meet with confidence; others want personalized service that requires special attention; still others confront you with problems that challenge your patience and skills.

What Causes Stress?

Deadlines, delivery dates, paperwork, and challenging customers are normal in any work environment. Pressure and tension build as a result of trying to meet the many demands of your job. Some people can tolerate more stress than others. It is important to identify what causes you to feel stress so that you can develop a plan to deal with it. Some common sources of stress include:

- People (customers, your boss).
- Lack of knowledge (product).
- Lack of support or direction.
- Unrealistic demands.
- Unclear goals.
- Conflicting priorities.
- Fear of the unknown.

Everyone Reacts Differently

A certain amount of stress can help you to be your best, but too much can affect your ability to provide excellent customer service. Each person reacts differently to stress.

Think about your current position.

What creates stress for you on the job?

_____

_____

_____

_____

_____

How does stress make you feel?

_____

_____

_____

_____

_____

What do you do to relieve your feelings of stress?

_____

_____

_____

_____

_____

Dealing with Stress

Some of the stress factors you listed can be controlled; others can be eliminated or ignored. You have learned several techniques in this book that will help you deal with customers and problem situations you may encounter on the job. With practice, these strategies can reduce the level of stress you feel. But some stress is normal and developing a plan to deal with it can improve your effectiveness on the job. Try some of the following stress relievers to find the ones that work for you.

Stress Relievers

- Change your routine: do things differently to relieve monotony; rearrange your environment (move furniture around; decorate with plants or photographs).
- Practice relaxation exercises: breath deeply; stretch your muscles; learn yoga.
- Take a physical break: go for a brisk walk; swim; play tennis; learn a new sport; join a health club.
- Take up a hobby: learn a foreign language; take music lessons; learn to cook Chinese, Mexican, or Italian food; take an arts and crafts course.
- Use your support network: spend time with family and friends; join a support group; ask your doctor to recommend tips for relieving stress.
- Above all, leave your job at work—don't take it home with you.

When Customers Upset You.   When a particularly difficult customer upsets you, don't take it personally. Customers bring their emotions to their encounters with you. Learn to step back mentally, and remember that to the customer you are the company, not an individual with feelings and emotions. Customers may call you names, threaten you, or promise to seek revenge. You must struggle to retain your professionalism. Resist responding in a similar manner. There will be time after the customer is gone to deal with your own emotions.

After the Customer Leaves.   When the customer leaves, you can, and should, take time to regroup. Take a break, go for a walk, or call a friend. At the very least, count to 10 and take several deep breaths. You do not want to approach the next customer with a bad feeling from the previous encounter. Congratulate yourself for remaining calm and cool under pressure. Talk to a friend or colleague who has had a similar experience. Take heart. Not all customers are alike. Sometimes you will have to endure an unpleasant encounter, but many more times you will be able to take pleasure in having helped your customers.

Examine What Happened.   Take time to examine what happened and learn from it. Review the encounter mentally and focus on what you did well. Don't beat yourself up for mistakes you think you made. Use them to plan how you will do things differently in the future. Every encounter, good or bad, will teach you something. Don't abandon your new skills when you run into some difficulty. Practice will indeed make perfect.

Use the following chart to review customer encounters—those that go well and those that do not—to help you improve your skills.

CUSTOMER ENCOUNTER REVIEW SHEET

	Things I Did Well	Things I Could Do Differently
Greeting		
Probing		
Body language		
Forming a partnership with the customer		
Voice tone and pitch		
Analyzing the alternatives		
Gaining the customer's commitment		

6

▮ R e v i e w   &   P r a c t i c e

Chu Tze Chou walks over to the desk where Kesner Pierre, an account manager, is sitting. Kesner stands and says, "Good morning. How may I help you today?" and offers Chu Tze a seat.

"Well," Chu Tze begins, "I just got this notice in the mail that you are going to close my account. I maintain the required minimum balance and I've never bounced a check. What's the story?"

"Let me check into that for you," Kesner replies, taking the letter and bringing up the account records on his computer. "I see from your account history that for the last eight months you have exceeded the maximum number of checks you can draw on this account. The Saverplus account is intended to be more of a savings account than a checking account. Keeping high minimum balances and low activity on the account allows us to give you the highest rate of interest on your money. Do you have a regular checking account with us?"

"No. Why did you give me checks with this account if you don't want me to use them? Interest rates are low enough at this bank. Go ahead, close the account. I'll take my money to a bank that wants my business!" Chu Tze declares loudly. ▮

What facts does Kesner have to support saying no to this customer?

_____
_____
_____

What alternatives could Kesner offer the customer?

_____
_____
_____

What can Kesner say or do to close the encounter effectively?

_____
_____
_____

What did Kesner do well during the encounter with Chu Tze?

_____

_____

_____

What could Kesner have done differently to improve the situation?

_____

_____

_____

6

Chapter Checkpoints

✓ Personalize your customer closings.

✓ Remember to thank your customers for their business.

✓ Be firm but gentle when saying no to a customer.

✓ Remain calm, use the facts, and offer alternatives when the answer is no.

✓ Always end politely, even when the customer leaves you upset.

✓ Recognize what causes stress for you on the job and find ways to relieve stress.

✓ Take the time to review your customer encounters and learn from your mistakes.

7 | A Plan for Action

This chapter will help you to:

- Assess your customer service skills.
- Prepare a plan of action to improve your skills.

HOW DO I RATE?

Use the following survey to assess your customer service skills. Circle the number under the response that best rates how you work with customers. When you complete the survey, read the directions for scoring.

	Always	Often	Some-times	Rarely	Never
1. I understand my responsibilities to my customers.	1	2	3	4	5
2. I make an effort to build partner-ships with work associates.	1	2	3	4	5
3. I strive to meet customer expec-tations.	1	2	3	4	5
4. I know who my customers are and what they need.	1	2	3	4	5
5. I listen when my customers complain.	1	2	3	4	5
6. I understand how needs affect behavior.	1	2	3	4	5
7. I create positive customer encounters.	1	2	3	4	5
8. I focus on the instances of impact.	1	2	3	4	5
9. I don't let my personal emotions get in the way of my work.	1	2	3	4	5
10. I make my customers feel good.	1	2	3	4	5

	Always	Often	Some-times	Rarely	Never
11. I know how to determine what my customers need.	1	2	3	4	5
12. I ask open questions to get good information from my customers.	1	2	3	4	5
13. I know the features of my products and/or services.	1	2	3	4	5
14. I discuss the benefits of my products and/or services with my customers.	1	2	3	4	5
15. I appreciate the tangible and intangible losses my customers may experience and try to minimize them.	1	2	3	4	5
16. I use positive body language when dealing with my customers.	1	2	3	4	5
17. I use my voice tone and inflection to communicate with my customers.	1	2	3	4	5
18. I choose words that my customers will understand.	1	2	3	4	5
19. I actively listen to my customers and demonstrate my interest in them.	1	2	3	4	5
20. I communicate effectively over the telephone.	1	2	3	4	5
21. I acknowledge problems that customers bring to my attention.	1	2	3	4	5
22. I seek information and ask questions to clarify problems.	1	2	3	4	5
23. I let the customer know I understand the problem.	1	2	3	4	5
24. I look for alternative solutions to problems with my customers.	1	2	3	4	5
25. I always follow up with customers who have problems.	1	2	3	4	5
26. I personalize my customer closings.	1	2	3	4	5
27. I remember to thank my customers for their business.	1	2	3	4	5
28. I am firm, but gentle, when saying no to a customer.	1	2	3	4	5
29. I remain calm, use the facts, and offer alternatives when I tell a customer no.	1	2	3	4	5
30. I always end politely, even when the customer leaves me upset.	1	2	3	4	5

	Always	Often	Some-times	Rarely	Never
31. I know what causes me stress on the job.	1	2	3	4	5
32. I use positive techniques to relieve my stress.	1	2	3	4	5
33. I take the time to review my customer encounters and learn from my mistakes.	1	2	3	4	5

Directions for scoring: Add up the points in each column; then add across the bottom to get your total score.

SCORING KEY

If You Scored . . .	Then You . . .
50 or less	Are a real service professional.
51–92	Provide good service, but need to polish some of your skills.
93–129	Need to strengthen your weak points.
130–165	Need to read this book again.

7

HOW DO I IMPROVE MY SKILLS?

Use the results of the previous self-assessment to identify five skills (ones you rated yourself as three or higher) you want to work on. Use the following guide to prepare a plan of action. Identify each skill, what action you will take to improve it, and the dates you plan to start and finish your improvement process.

CUSTOMER SERVICE SKILLS ACTION PLAN

Skill	Action Needed	Start	End
1. _____	_____		
_____	_____		
_____	_____		
_____	_____		

Skill	Action Needed	Start	End
2.			
3.			
4.			
5.			

ONGOING IMPROVEMENT

Once you have successfully improved the first five skills, identify the remaining areas you want to improve and prepare another action plan for those skills. Return to the self-assessment survey periodically to rate your skills. When you attain a score of 50 or less, you will have reached your goal—to be a real service professional. In addition, use the Skill Maintenance Checklist on the inside back cover to ensure that your skills are kept sharp over the next year and throughout your career.

7

Post-Test

Test your mastery of the material by circling the best answer to the following questions.

1. The best way to handle a customer who enters my place of business with fire in his or her eyes is to:

    a. Turn and walk the other way.

    b. Signal my supervisor immediately.

    c. Approach the customer with a smile and ask how I may help.

    d. Wait until we are face-to-face to ask what might be the problem.

2. Most customers who have product or service complaints:

    a. Confront the manager with the issue immediately.

    b. Never complain, but take their business elsewhere.

    c. Write scathing letters to management after the fact.

    d. Continue to use the product or service, but demand retribution.

3. Customers who encounter poor service or unmet expectations usually:

    a. Refrain from discussing it with others.

    b. Share their story with one or two close associates.

    c. Record the incidence on paper to refer to later.

    d. Tell as many as 8 other people about their bad experience.

4. Ninety-five percent of your customers whose product or service problems are resolved to their satisfaction quickly will:

    a. Take their business elsewhere anyway.

    b. Continue to do business with you.

c. Comparison shop your competitors looking for a better deal.

d. Refer others to your place of business.

5. What is the primary reason that customers discontinue doing business with a particular company or organization?

a. Price of product or service.

b. Dissatisfaction with the product.

c. Employee indifference or attitude.

d. Inconvenient location.

6. In terms of dollars and cents, a company will spend _____ attracting new customers than it needs to keep existing customers.

a. 10 times more

b. 6 times more

c. 2 times more

d. The same amount

7. A customer who brings a problem to my attention is looking for:

a. Heads to roll.

b. Something for nothing.

c. Someone to listen, understand, and solve the problem.

d. All of the above.

8. The problems that customers bring to my attention are almost always:

a. Due to a lack of communication.

b. My fault.

c. Due to a computer error.

d. Their fault.

9. Difficult situations with customers usually involve a customer:

a. Who has a special request.

b. Who cannot make up his or her mind.

c. Who is angry or defensive.

d. Who is all of the above.

10. Listening to product or service complaints can:

a. Build better customer relations.

b. Improve quality.

c. Increase market share and profits.

d. Do all of the above.

10. **d**

1. **c**   2. **b**   3. **d**   4. **b**   5. **c**   6. **b**   7. **c**   8. **a**   9. **d**

ANSWER KEY

The Business Skills Express Series

This growing series of books addresses a broad range of key business skills and topics to meet the needs of employees, human resource departments, and training consultants.

To obtain information about these and other Business Skills Express books, please call McGraw-Hill toll free at: 1-800-2-McGRAW.

Effective Performance Management
ISBN   1-55623-867-3

Hiring the Best
ISBN   1-55623-865-7

Writing that Works
ISBN   1-55623-856-8

Customer Service Excellence
ISBN   1-55623-969-6

Writing for Business Results
ISBN   1-55623-854-1

Powerful Presentation Skills
ISBN   1-55623-870-3

Meetings that Work
ISBN   1-55623-866-5

Effective Teamwork
ISBN   1-55623-880-0

Time Management
ISBN   1-55623-888-6

Assertiveness Skills
ISBN   1-55623-857-6

Motivation at Work
ISBN   1-55623-868-1

Overcoming Anxiety at Work
ISBN   1-55623-869-X

Positive Politics at Work
ISBN   1-55623-879-7

Telephone Skills at Work
ISBN   1-55623-858-4

Managing Conflict at Work
ISBN   1-55623-890-8

The New Supervisor: Skills for Success
ISBN   1-55623-762-6

The *Americans with Disabilities Act:* What Supervisors Need to Know
ISBN   1-55623-889-4

Managing the Demands of Work and Home
ISBN   0-7863-0221-6

Effective Listening Skills
ISBN   0-7863-0102-4

Goal Management at Work
ISBN   0-7863-0225-9

Positive Attitudes at Work
ISBN   0-7863-0167-8

Supervising the Difficult Employee
ISBN   0-7863-0219-4

Cultural Diversity in the Workplace
ISBN   0-7863-0125-2

Managing Change in the Workplace
ISBN   0-7863-0162-7

Negotiating for Business Results
ISBN   0-7863-0114-7

Practical Business Communication
ISBN   0-7863-0227-5

High-Performance Speaking
ISBN   0-7863-0222-4

Delegation Skills
ISBN   0-7863-0148-1

Coaching Skills: A Guide for Supervisors
ISBN   0-7863-0220-8

Customer Service and the Telephone
ISBN   0-7863-0224-0

Creativity at Work
ISBN   0-7863-0223-2

Effective Interpersonal Relationships
ISBN   0-7863-0255-0

The Participative Leader
ISBN   0-7863-0252-6

Building Customer Loyalty
ISBN   0-7863-0253-4

Getting and Staying Organized
ISBN   0-7863-0254-2

Total Quality Selling
ISBN   0-7863-0324-7

Business Etiquette
ISBN   0-7863-0323-9

Empowering Employees
ISBN   0-7863-0314-X

Training Skills for Supervisors
ISBN   0-7863-0313-1

Moving Meetings
ISBN   0-7863-0333-6

Multicultural Customer Service
ISBN   0-7863-0332-8